D0846273

Geography Zone: Landforms™

Exploring GLACIERS

Melody S. Mis

PowerKiDS
press.

New York

To Christine and Bryan Sullivan

Published in 2009 by The Rosen Publishing Group, Inc.
29 East 21st Street, New York, NY 10010

Copyright © 2009 by The Rosen Publishing Group, Inc.

All rights reserved. No part of this book may be reproduced in any form without permission in writing from the publisher, except by a reviewer.

First Edition

Editor: Nicole Pristash
Book Design: Julio Gil
Photo Researcher: Jessica Gerweck

Photo Credits: Cover, pp. 5, 7, 9, 11, 15, 19, 21 Shutterstock.com; p. 13 Image Courtesy of Earth Sciences and Image Analysis Laboratory, NASA Johnson Space Center; p. 17 © Michael Wheatley/AgeFotostock.

Library of Congress Cataloging-in-Publication Data

Mis, Melody S.
  Exploring glaciers / Melody S. Mis. — 1st ed.
      p. cm. — (Geography zone. Landforms)
  Includes index.
  ISBN 978-1-4358-2714-1 (library binding) — ISBN 978-1-4358-3112-4 (pbk.)
ISBN 978-1-4358-3118-6 (6-pack)
  1. Glaciers—Juvenile literature. 2. Glaciers—Alaska—Juvenile literature. 3. Extreme environments—Juvenile literature. I. Title.
  GB2403.8.M57 2009
  551.31'2—dc22
                                          2008026795

Manufactured in the United States of America

Contents

A glacier is a large **mass** of ice that moves very slowly. Glaciers form where the weather is cold, such as on the tops of high mountains, in Antarctica, and in the Arctic. Glaciers were even found on the **planet** Mars at one time!

A glacier is its own landform. However, did you know that glaciers also help form other landforms? As glaciers move, they can build up and **carve** out new landforms, such as hills and valleys, that you may see every day. Let's learn about the different types of glaciers and the ways they shape our Earth!

Today, glaciers cover around 10 percent of the land on Earth. Glaciers also store about 75 percent of the world's freshwater.

Did you know that glaciers begin as tiny snowflakes? When a lot of snowflakes fall on the ground, they make snow. When the snow does not melt, new snow stays on top of the old snow. As more snow falls, it builds up to form a large mass of ice that becomes a glacier.

Glaciers form at different rates. Some glaciers form in 10 years. Others take hundreds of thousands of years to form. The colder the weather is, the longer it takes to make a glacier. Ice sheets, for example, take a very long time to form.

Snow does not melt in places that are very cold. When this happens, snow and ice can build up and form glaciers, like this one.

Ice sheets are huge, flat glaciers that cover large pieces of land. They are the biggest glaciers on Earth. There are only two ice sheets in the world. They are in Greenland and Antarctica. The Antarctic ice sheet covers around 5.4 **million** square miles (14 million sq km). It is more than 2 miles (3 km) deep in some places!

Some people mix ice caps up with ice sheets. Ice caps cover large **areas**, too, but they are smaller than ice sheets. An ice cap is shaped like a dome or plate, and ice caps are considered to be mountain glaciers.

The Antarctic ice sheet, shown here, covers 98 percent of Antarctica. It is the largest mass of ice on Earth.

If you have ever seen snow on the top of a mountain, it may have been a mountain glacier. A mountain glacier forms on the top of a mountain, and the glacier then flows down into the mountain's valleys. People call mountain glaciers rivers of ice because they often flow down old riverbeds that have dried up.

Mountain glaciers are common. There are mountain glaciers in more than 40 countries. In the United States, mountain glaciers are found in the Rocky Mountains and in Alaska. There are also mountain glaciers in the Himalayas, in Asia, and the Alps, in Europe.

In between these mountains sits Mer de Glace Glacier. It is the longest glacier in France.

Tidewater glaciers are mountain glaciers that flow out to the ocean. When they reach the sea, part of the ice can fall off into the water. This broken piece is called an iceberg. Only around one-eighth of an iceberg shows above the water. The rest of the iceberg is heavier, so it stays underwater.

A piedmont glacier is a mountain glacier that spreads out like a fan when it reaches flat land. Malaspina Glacier, in Alaska, is one of the largest piedmont glaciers in the world. It is around 40 miles (65 km) wide and 28 miles (45 km) long.

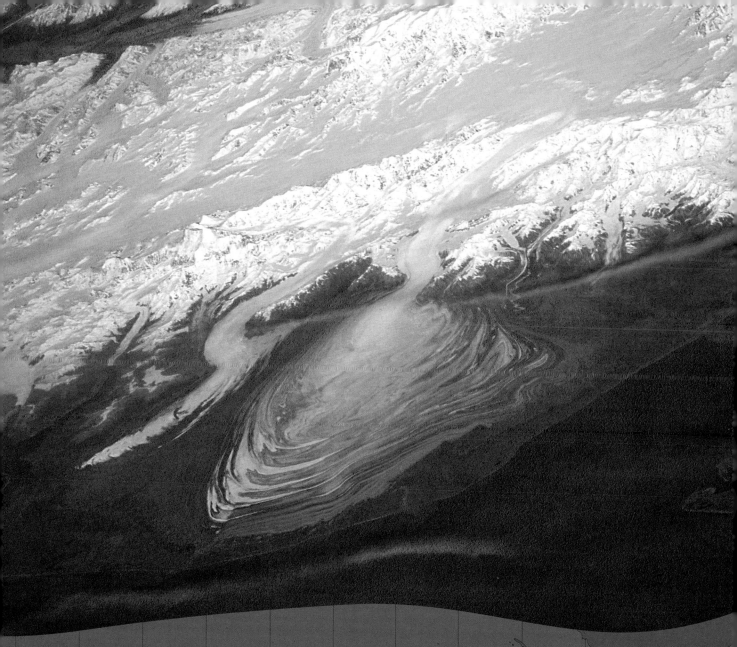

Malaspina Glacier, shown here, is so large that the whole glacier can be seen only from space. This picture was taken by the spacecraft *Endeavour*.

As glaciers move, they shape the **landscape** around us and form other landforms. One way glaciers form landforms is through **erosion**. When a glacier moves, it picks up rocks. These rocks then cut the land underneath the glacier as it moves. For example, U-shaped valleys are formed when a glacier moves in between mountains.

Another way glaciers shape Earth is through **deposition**. As a glacier moves or melts, it often leaves behind rocks and soil it picked up. The rocks and soil can build up over time and form hills. Some of these hills are called moraines and eskers.

This is a valley in Yosemite National Park, in California. Millions of years ago, glaciers helped carve the valley into the shape it has today.

Glaciers are very cold, so there are only a few **organisms** that can live right on them. Spiders and flies can be found on glaciers. However, they often become food for the birds that fly overhead. Snow **algae** live on glaciers, too. They are able to grow very well in the ice and snow.

Snow algae, though, are food for ice worms. The ice worm is a tiny worm about 1 inch (2.5 cm) long. It crawls inside glaciers during the day. Then, at night, the ice worm crawls to the top of the ice to find food.

Snow algae, shown here, can often look pink. Because of this, people call it watermelon snow. Watermelon is a sweet fruit that has a pink inside.

Some of the most beautiful glaciers in the world are found in Alaska. There are more than 100,000 mountain glaciers, piedmont glaciers, and tidewater glaciers there.

Two of Alaska's most famous glaciers are Hubbard Glacier and Columbia Glacier. Hubbard Glacier is the largest tidewater glacier in North America. It is 76 miles (122 km) long. Columbia Glacier is one of the fastest-moving glaciers in the world. In 2001, it moved around 98 feet (30 m) per day.

Many animals and plants make their homes near and around Alaska's beautiful glaciers. People live in this area as well.

Here you can see a boat getting up close to Hubbard Glacier.
Many of Alaska's glaciers are studied and visited by people.

Some glaciers do not have much life around them. However, this is not true in Alaska. Animals, such as bears, moose, and wolves, live in the forests near Alaska's glaciers. People live near them, too. In fact, people called Eskimos were the first people to make Alaska's glaciers their home.

Life around Alaska's glaciers can be hard. The weather is cold, and there are very few roads. Small planes take people and supplies to faraway villages. Some people use **dogsleds** to get from place to place. Even though it can be hard, living near glaciers can be fun, too.

These seals are resting on pieces of ice near Meares Glacier, in Alaska.

Many people climb glaciers for sport. Others fish or boat near them, too. However, warmer weather is causing some glaciers to melt. This is bad because many animals that live on or near glaciers could lose their homes. Some say people are to blame. Our cars and factories put bad gases into the air, and these gases are causing the warmer weather.

People are learning more ways to keep our air as clean as possible, though. You can learn about them at school or on the Internet. Then, you can help keep glaciers safe for a long time!

algae (AL-jee) Plantlike living things without stems that live in water.

areas (ER-ee-uz) Certain places.

carve (KAHRV) To cut into a shape.

deposition (deh-puh-ZIH-shun) The dropping of tiny bits of rock in a new place.

dogsleds (DOG-sledz) Carts on which people ride that are pulled by dogs.

erosion (ih-ROH-zhun) The wearing away of land over time.

landscape (LAND-skayp) The landforms, such as hills, mountains, and valleys, in a place.

mass (MAS) The amount of matter in things.

million (MIL-yun) One thousand thousands.

organisms (OR-guh-nih-zumz) Living beings made of dependent parts.

planet (PLA-net) A large object, such as Earth, that moves around the Sun.

A
Antarctica, 4, 8
Arctic, 4

D
deposition, 14
dogsleds, 20

E
Earth, 4, 8, 14
erosion, 14

G
Greenland, 8

H
hills, 4, 14

I
ice, 4, 6, 10, 12, 16
ice sheets, 6, 8

L
land, 8, 12, 14

M
Mars, 4
mass, 4, 6
mountain(s), 4, 10, 14

O
organisms, 16

S
snow, 6, 10, 16
snow algae, 16

V
valleys, 4, 10, 14

W
weather, 4, 6, 20, 22
world, 8, 12, 18

Web Sites

Due to the changing nature of Internet links, PowerKids Press has developed an online list of Web sites related to the subject of this book. This site is updated regularly. Please use this link to access the list:
www.powerkidslinks.com/gzone/glacier/

3 1125 00684 3443